TOUGH SKIN

Sarah Eaton

TOUGH SKIN

Sarah Eaton

BlazeVOX [books]

Buffalo, New York

TOUGH SKIN
by Sarah Eaton

Copyright © 2010

Published by BlazeVOX [books]

Printed in the United States of America

Book design by Geoffrey Gatza
Cover art by Sarah Jackson-Moore

First Edition
ISBN: 9781935402619
Library of Congress Control Number 2009910014

BlazeVOX [books]
303 Bedford Ave
Buffalo, NY 14216

Editor@blazevox.org

publisher of weird little books

BlazeVOX [books]

blazevox.org

2   4   6   8   0   9   7   5   3   1

B   X

Contents

TOUGH SKIN

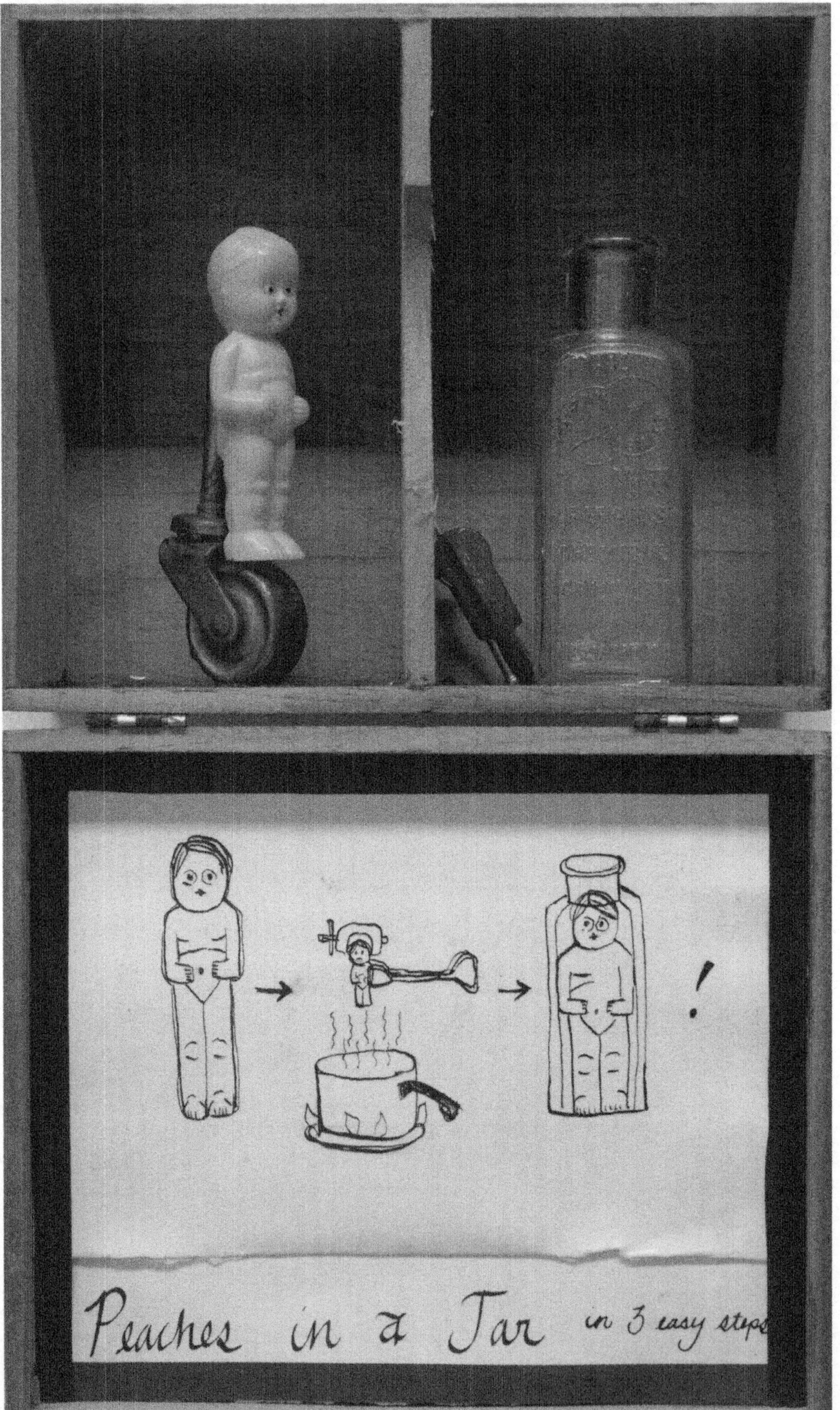
Peaches in a Jar in 3 easy steps

What I Claim as my Invention

Part One:

The time-traveling inventor alternately contemplates suicide and torture while his blood baby slumps unattractively.

Duty Spurts. It is not my fault.

Be it forever known that your protection has been foremost in my mind; these hands guided by blond toddlers, this mouth, unseeing, seeks no rewards. From one orifice to the next, your best interests are mine.
It is not my fault those interests dip to the gaping crevices between stitches in the seams.

My intent remains, unwaveringly: To *prevent any looseness of the jaws even after long continued use*[1]. Duty doesn't always call.

Sometimes it spurts or jerks. Sometimes it burns.

Delicate, as have I often heard the skin revered. Also animal soft. Also hot. Scarring reduces sensitivity. Fire victims, overwhelmingly, have less than satisfactory intimate connections. Someone did a study once.

Your mother told me it would do you good to be a little less sensitive, but she is a cruel woman, and I am not about to start listening to her.

Flinch not away from my blue flame.

---

[1] E Pietz et al Forceps, Filed April 15, 1922 (1,510,416)

Worms Plus Oatmeal

Teeth are the last thing I need coming at me. The first: To *close blood vessels*, to *prevent bleeding.*[2]
Letting of blood is still fashionable, but in the future leeches will become novelty delicacies, gently sucking the tongues of epicures before sliding esophageal-wise.

A certain degree of relative play[3] is expected. So let's hop to it, Peaches.

This pinches and spreads, much like fingers, except colder. I like mine hard, you like yours soft; luckily, for every aesthetic there is a metal.
Ours is lead.

Your *unbeveled face*[4] haunts me. Most people have cheekbones, or at least a nose.

For all my inventioneering, I could never make you seem as others might, though I've learned far more about the human brain than I may have otherwise by shining candlelight up your unobscured nostrils.

It is gray. It looks like worms plus oatmeal. It shivers when you poke it with a stick.

Here's something irritating about the future, Peaches: Rats become pets.
And, if you even casually mention to someone in the health care profession that you've contemplated suicide, they will totally come at you with government agents.

Apparently there is no such thing as "sort of suicidal." You is or you ain't. *Slipping will be positively prevented.*[5]

---

[2] E Pietz et al Forceps, Filed April 15, 1922 (1,510,416)
[3] Ibid.
[4] Ibid.
[5] Ibid.

My Skittery Moon Pie's Scalp Oozes Gold

In the future, there is something called self-esteem. Ever so fragile, ever so light, it's almost like a soul or something else imaginary.

Humans are *hollow in construction*[6]; there is a lot of air in there, and at the center spins a single onyx orb.

Render *the ball sluggish*[7]. Then get busy with some pincers and a blow torch.

Blow torches are from the future, dear.
Common uses include carmelizing brulées and searing off faces.

Shrink not away, my skittery moon pie.
The roughening might be omitted[8], depending strictly on the efficacy of my potion.
Elixirs I have eschewed in the past, disparaging them as the tools of crazy-coiffed beaker fanatics. But, a certain ringletted floozie twisted my arm, and here we are.

Drink it or I'll pour it up your nose.

Expect this: *These pimples are distributed all over the surface*[9] of your scalp. No one will be able to see or feel them but you. The best part is, when squeezed, these pimples ooze molten gold covered in pus. To uncover the gold, simply roll the pus ball around in your cheek until it tastes more tangy than salty. Et voila.

---

[6] W L Eaton Practice Golf Ball, Filed May 4, 1922 (1,483,165)

[7] Ibid.

[8] Ibid.

[9] Ibid.

Might Mean Something Else Entirely

I would never drive another to suicide. Would it be just as bad to watch your old da
use his toe as index finger and splat his way onto wallpaper? Forget it.
Be it *gutta-percha, rubber, celluloid, wood, or treated paper*[10], your silly poppy
makes a better addition as an absence.

Besides, I have never met a rifle that can best me.

I wish to inflict.

Pop those zits, suck those globes, drop that gold. Now, run across the little beads; it
will conjure such a humorous tableau. Peaches, you look like a lollipop with wheels
for legs!

My ticker, my cage; methinks it's high blood pressure. That's what happens when
people pump this cuff around your bicep tight, and then you get the wrong
numbers. Watch out, and it might happen to you, too, one day.

But you bruise easily. That might mean something else entirely. Like cancer.

Here: *Practice swinging the club*[11]. Your muscles may have atrophied, but I have to
tell you, I am downright excited about death, be it mine or yours or anyone else's.

The future doesn't hold any answers as to whether we float on clouds or flames lick
our secret places or nothingness or whatever. Oh, there is speculation aplenty. Of
all kinds. About everything. In the future.

But, irreverence protects us.

---

[10] W L Eaton Practice Golf Ball, Filed May 4, 1922 (1,483,165)
[11] Ibid.

Your Countenance Resembled Slime

Have I told you the story of your conception? Each child should know the miracle of union. You were *made in such a manner*[12] that we presupposed our coupling should produce one *retarded, and* one *therefore* that *does not travel far*[13].

Not only were we upside-down and backwards, but also inside-out. Our capillaries joined and suckled, eventually spitting up what I came to refer to as a blood baby.

Initially, your countenance resembled slime. In other hands you would have been miscarriage, but I know the truth. The answer is…Nurture!

Sans loving soul kisses and needle and thread, you would have been pulp. And pulp hasn't consciousness. A dog would have eaten you. You would have preferred it?

Let me tell you a story: In the future, chickens beaks will be sliced off with a red hot soldering iron so they do not peck their own flesh and the flesh of others held in close quarters, but it is far, far better that those chickens were allowed to breathe their breaths.

Whether they could not eat, whether they became food themselves. You are a beakless chicken, Peaches, but you are alive. You are *strong enough to stand up under the usage to which* you are *to be put.*[14]

---

[12] W L Eaton Practice Golf Ball, Filed May 4, 1922 (1,483,165)
[13] Ibid.
[14] Ibid.

Detoxification Requires Commitment

Like all beings, you are limited. I've found a way to push past what might have caused others to wallow and slow, but to nudge you to this point would only cause your muscles to snap and your limbs hang useless.

This is the time when we are both tested. Some might say by God, but you and I both know God does not interfere.

This is when we ascertain the degree of trust that hovers betwixt us. You were made by me, and I shall unmake you. However, not right now.

Trust me?

The wet mop is inserted.[15] Relax your throat, allow the cloth tentacles to massage cilia and membrane alike. This is an ancient preparatory practice.

You bathe your skin once a year; what makes you think your other organs should escape scrubbing? Unfortunately, it is not so easy as a deadened gag reflex and a double-hinged jaw. How will we ever reach your liver?

---

[15] F A Eaton Mop Wringer, Filed April 10, 1922 (1,452,798)

Neither Innie nor Outie

Another tale: You were born a glob.

Construction ensued. Your mother spoke of dolls and panels screwed. She treated you as porcelain because you were, partly.

After your making, she achieved nothing but sadness. A woman once proud to stand behind podiums, unafraid to speak nonsense or enter into fisticuffs, she stooped over you, removing *a back that slides as a whole*[16], ladeling waste and nutrition in and out by turns, you resting on your belly sighing with contentment.

For her, not you, I stitched skin. I made a costume to bring her back and ease the burden that was a child so breakable.

For her, not you, I excavated and stripped, I undid dones and chose only the supplest flesh. She insisted that I take care with your torso, that your "brain" be lovingly encased, that *greater pressure on the upper part*[17] would result in harm.

Frankly—don't take this the wrong way—it might have been better if my *incomplete and ununiform*[18] sewing failed. Long story short: You don't have a liver.

Nor, my dear, have you sexual organs. I think of you as a girl because you are weak. So when I see *a shaft is journalled*[19] in your sketchpad, I think it appropriate, sweetie. You are neither innie, nor outie, but it's only natural that you make attempts to shoehorn your "self," as it were, into the constructs of society.

I will obscure your vision with black muslin, and things will become easier for you, Peaches.

---

[16] F A Eaton Mop Wringer, Filed April 10, 1922 (1,452,798)
[17] Ibid.
[18] Ibid.
[19] Ibid.

No Self-respecting Fox Would Wear a Nurse's Cap

I blame your mother. When she passed on, I really thought I was free to pursue all kinds of mad scientist-type activities, but the more tears I shed, the less I thought about cutting off your head and putting it in a jar.

Had I everything to do all over again, these are the things I would change: you, me, your mother.

The art of dressing you has always eluded me. My urge to clothe you in burlap and hair shirts tends to overwhelm parental tenderness.

But not today, my sweet. You're drooling quite fetchingly. I shall drape you in *pervious walls through which the air can readily pass*[20].

You are like a worm, coiled and dried to jerky.
You are like a seafood salad made only of squid tentacles.

I shall dress you in mayonnaise and a light spritz of lemon. I shall drape around your neck an amulet of ink that releases on contact.

Peaches, it is only so I will know if your lips have traversed beyond the cage that holds them. Lips touch, blood spills, attraction/repulsion; next thing you know knickers are everywhere but on your bum.

Even if you're *fragmentarily indicated, the curtains being rolled up in open position*[21], males lap and yowl at anything that resembles meat.

---

[20] C Eaton Food Safe, Filed April 4, 1922 (1,411,272)
[21] Ibid.

You Are Seriously Unattractive

Have you the patience for one more tale? I always dreamed to sire a fox instead of a child.

They're almost certainly the missing link between cats and dogs, and, though I have not had the pleasure to observe one in close quarters, I quite suspect them of possessing cinnamon-scented saliva and a wild penchant for ripping out throats. I tremble.

Thusly, Peaches, you are *heavily loaded with articles of food* and *readily suspended from a tree*[22].

Logic follows: A fox with its canine appetite will be unable to resist you and shimmy up the trunk. Its feline nature will rise, and it will find itself quite unable to cogitate a solution for quitting the tree.

I swoop in, collect it, teach it to walk upright and wear adorable sailor suits.

It will be a vast improvement on you. I quite imagine that's something every father has said to his child at one point or another; there's no need to look so downtrodden.

Injury will likely be incurred. Foxes are nippy. I am anticipating blood. *The sack* in which you are clothed is *thus constructed* that it *may be readily laundered*[23]. Also, I won't have to climb the tree to get you down, due to the *downward collapsing of the floor*[24] of your cage. Tent. Tent.

I will catch you as you fall. I will suckle you. I will perch upon your canid brother's head a nurse's cap, and he shall sit beside you, occasionally raising a vixen's wail as you drift in and out of existence.

No self-respecting fox would wear a nurse's cap. No creature would ever find you attractive enough to come close enough to catch.

---

[22] C Eaton Food Safe, Filed April 4, 1922 (1,411,272)
[23] Ibid.
[24] Ibid.

This Den Is Closed

Inserted through the open end[25], I have placed sustenance.

You may feed on this combination of honey comb, scrapple, and matchsticks for enough time. *Flies and other insects cannot have access to the interior*[26].

I encourage you to push your limits. In the future, average people will run marathons. The very short will outfit their automobiles so they might see over the wheel.

If that means setting a timer to remind you to irrigate your facial openings, so be it.

It could be complicated as becoming seamstress to your own wounds. It could be simple as ceasing to be.

You've always been opinionated, which has led me to believe you are alive. But it's no different than believing one's stuffed doll has love in its sawdust heart for its owner just because it does not fall off the bed in the night.

There are theories about energy transfer, but that is naught but mystical folderol.

My blood baby, my miscarriage, my stinky pile: I have cared for you.

And now I have pulled dirt over the opening and jumped vigorously on the earth to collapse the tunnel.

This den is closed.

---

[25] C Eaton Food Safe, Filed April 4, 1922 (1,411,272)
[26] Ibid.

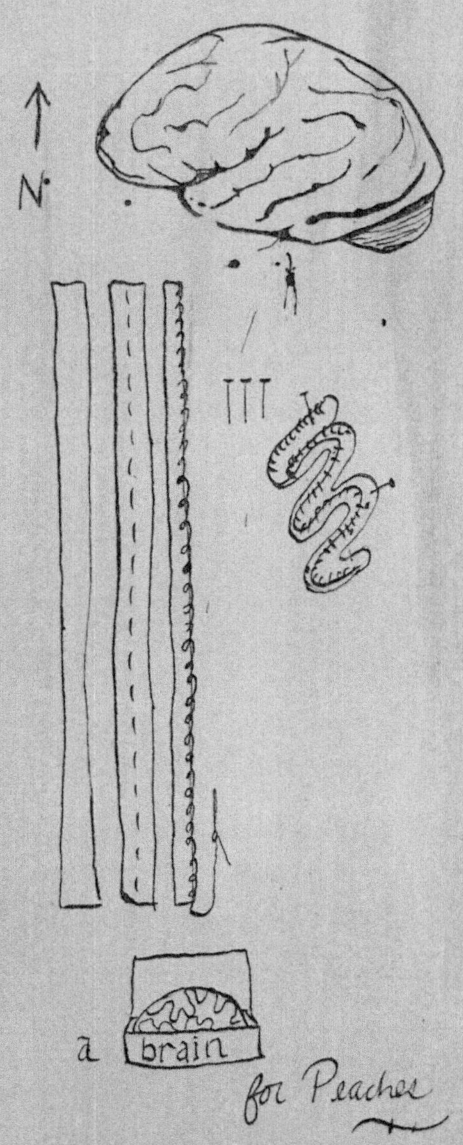
N
a brain
for Peaches

Part Two:

The time-traveling inventor attempts to justify his continued life at the ceasing of
the unattractive, but consistent, Peaches.

It's almost like I invented love.

To think of things that have not been thought I must loosen my associations,
observe the spaces between leaves, express myself only with inappropriate
body language.

The number of times I have been chased down by straitjackets surpasses the number
of times I have been stalked by naughty nurses.
I invite it. I feel something on my skin.

What would happen if no one had invented the kitchen match? The bamboo mat?
The horse? What if we never knew the properties of hoarhound?

Everyone would be perched atop feather cushions bemoaning their grape-bunch
hemorrhoids, that's what. Their tastebuds would rot and drop off like so many
sequins.

Inaccurate gustatory experiences aside, my mouth fizz has lately taken on the
consistency of mortar.

In the future, invention is about improvement. It almost always involves tweezers
and an advanced degree. I don't want to shoot small animals into space; I want to
shoot people.

Did you know that I invented the wedding ring? Without it: rampant sexual
collision. Also spoons with jagged edges for eating grapefruit.

If I hadn't invented the intercom and the binoculars, I could have slipped away so
easily. If I hadn't invented the elixir against scarlet fever.
If I had invented disappearing without death.

I can't stop.
That which is legendary has intertwined with truth. Are you asleep yet?
Euphemisms often accompany euthanasia. The plane of your cranium puts me in
mind of billiards. I vacillate between smacking you with my bare hands or with my
bare feet.

I can't stop, Peaches. Dead or alive, your pulpy familiarity rests comfortably as my
tongue's target. Dead or alive, there is not much difference between what once was
and what is.

Perhaps I am a sentimental being after all.

What I claim as my invention: You. Me.

Who will sweep behind me?

Crippling bowel cramps. Puny musculature. Flat cookies. Shiny cheeks. Bloody noses. Vein obstruction. Naked donuts. Scattershot.

Not everything is meant to be a liquid, or viscous, or some other in-between state, *solid or hollow or made for example of wood, metal, ivory, or vulcanized rubber*[27]. Sometimes a loose brushing achieves the desired effect. Also, at what point can a handful be categorized as sand, or, in the other direction, dust?

What I claim as my invention: It does not naturally occur. It is not a part of the body (sleep is moist). Wet subtraction leads to ridges, flakes, platelets, and ash. Kissing cousins, certainly, but not an exact match. It is *especially intended for use by ladies when a maid is not present.*[28]

Peaches would have mourned the animals' crushed bones, but lapped at the beige mounds when my attention turned elsewhere, storing protein, hardening cartilage, mortaring, pestling.

Arid lab conditions would have forced swaddled tongues and sweatbands *of suede kid or chamois leather, or silver, or of any other suitable material*[29]. The image that bumps aside sexual fantasies as I lie on the cusp of oblivion: Her glossal nudgings into my life's work.

Am I mourning?

Breaking something down is harder than it seems. My measurement: It is fine enough if granular differentiation is impossible. I define impossible. Therefore, success and laziness intertwine and complement each other. Nothing is more satisfying than reaching goals. It *renders the user's grasp…more secure*[30].

Could it be the creaks and scrapes heard throughout the lab never should have been attributed to your pathetic shufflings? Did they belong to a ghost cat or nature itself? Hallucination may be a daily reality, but I know what I know.

You are deader than ash. You are the ground stone of your namesake. You are powder.

---

[27] H Ericson-Smith Toilet Powder Applying Device or Implement, Filed Oct. 10, 1922 (1,431,881)
[28] Ibid.
[29] Ibid.
[30] Ibid.

Everyone knows what commingled barking means

I am proud of your legacy, Peaches. Nearly everything you did required rescue, *winding engagement therewith in the usual manner*[31]. It makes your pop puff up with gas acquired from celebrating his own achievements by consuming rich meats and foamy lager. I boast between bites: I took her down from here; I brought her home from there; dangling by a synapse, this close to a time machine.

Without brakes I would have leaped so far forward that it would just be me and an ancient chimpanzee floating like fairy bugs through impenetrable darkness, our lungs collapsed, our eyes bulged. Everything ends.

Without brakes I never would have spied my woman supine and submissive beneath my collection of young male jungle cats. Their commingled barking gave enough indication. Swamp lynx she was.

I did what any violent cuckold might and endeavored to *press them against the treads with great force*[32]. Make no mistake, my insensate spawn, my mind leaps to the worst case scenario without much prompting—something that causes regrets aplenty in a weaker man.

I never saw them again, but sometimes, when the thumping, howling recesses of my interior dwellings grew oppressive I retreated to the veranda and imagined their vengeance. Now quiet, pushed by cruelty to untrod resources, pencils shoved between paw pads, outlining their murderous intentions on slabs of sand, they thought only of me, not her.

It is not just people who will hurt you. It is everything. It is animals and fish. It is plants. It is water. It is air. When one windmills one's arm by one's side, disturbing the breeze, does that truly upset the air? Can I tender revenge against everything?

I have the time. Pinching atoms, kicking violets, munching on handfuls of nails: I will project my pain by inflicting it. You should feel pleased to have departed.

---

[31] HI Wrigley Hand Brake Mechanism, Filed Aug. 2, 1922 (1,518,724)
[32] Ibid.

If you don't skate downhill, I will shove you

You led me to believe in my own abilities to conjure something from nothing, even if something's definition was hazy.

To be a tree, asexually populating the ground; to be a hippie, grinding against that tree. A hippie is from the future, dearest. Oh, I forget. You know everything now. Have you seen God yet? Does He know who I am?

Although I have tracked my annoyance and irritability using hatchmarks of differing lengths to signify severity for the last decade, I was unprepared for this maelstrom of indifference that has arisen. You were *simply a preferred embodiment of the invention*[33].

So what? I can make another pile of oozing grotesquerie.
I could do it right now; I just don't want to.

They spoke of you in the village as my simpleton pet. Children's eyeballs burned to liquid at the sight of you. Astigmatic elders referred to you as the lumpen bore, and me as the odd fellow who *keeps said bore clear of all matter*[34], so cautious was I that no leaf, no dustlet, no chipmunk, wafted and adhered to your skin coverings.

That is, I suppose, a kind of love.
All I ever wanted for you was *openings to permit manipulation and inspection*[35].
It's all any father wants: his child to skate always downhill, and it is so much easier simply to do and be what other people want.

If there is any hurting to be done, I want it *to be maintained sterile until used*[36].
Emotion clogs.

---

[33] HS Cook Aseptic Needle Holder, Filed March 2, 1922 (1,694,768)
[34] Ibid.
[35] Ibid.
[36] Ibid.

I manmade art. I manmade life.

Sometimes art is cruel. If you never realize this, you will never be great. You will also never be alone. Do you think your friends are your legacy?

Today I tasted a sweet almond and dozed under a vision of sugared esculent morsels. You were not sweet. You were not bitter.

What is something that is neither one thing nor the other? How can one be great if one is not recognized? It is possible. It is possible.

How to, how to: Maybe I am slightly poisoned already, maybe one more small dose is the single action between me and whatever it is that accompanies death. But the saporous jolt means only unpleasantness before oblivion. Perhaps I desire a capsule, perhaps another way out. It is worldly: Death without pain, extinction accompanying serenity. Not knowing. I want to do something to myself without knowing that I am doing it to myself. If anyone can do it, it is I.

I have never been late—I am possessed of a time machine—but I have squandered time as a result. I neglected to permanently postulate my theories. I did not submit patent requests. Paperwork is the devil's very hooves. Everything that I've invented shall be recreated.

The late inventor, they will jabber. That odd man. The one who took away our pain with opiates. The one who ground our glass so finely it turned into something else entirely.

The one who had no effect whatsoever upon our lives other than as an object of gossip.

Today I tasted a bitter almond and wondered if this was it—if I had snuck backwards in time and dusted my afternoon snack with deadly powder. But my means for skipping about the seasons was never so accurate. The brakes squealed with each application, the frequency of such was enough to drive a man to build himself a child.

Rope, pistol, knife, blunt object: I invented them all. I twisted twine, but first I invented it by plucking individual coarse hairs from monkey tails. I spun. I invented the spinning wheel. I studied watchmaking. Buttons, hooks, zippers, pulleys, cloth of plant and animal, wire, elements: Put the word manmade in front of anything, and I manmade it.

…certain novel features of construction…
…move head foremost and turn on their backs…
…very simple and economical of construction…

...preferably made of metallic blades or other material of suitable stiffness...[37]

...defunct, late, lifeless, exanimate, demised...

---

[37] F. Heath Sardine Turning Apparatus, Filed Sept. 26, 1922 (1,430,011)

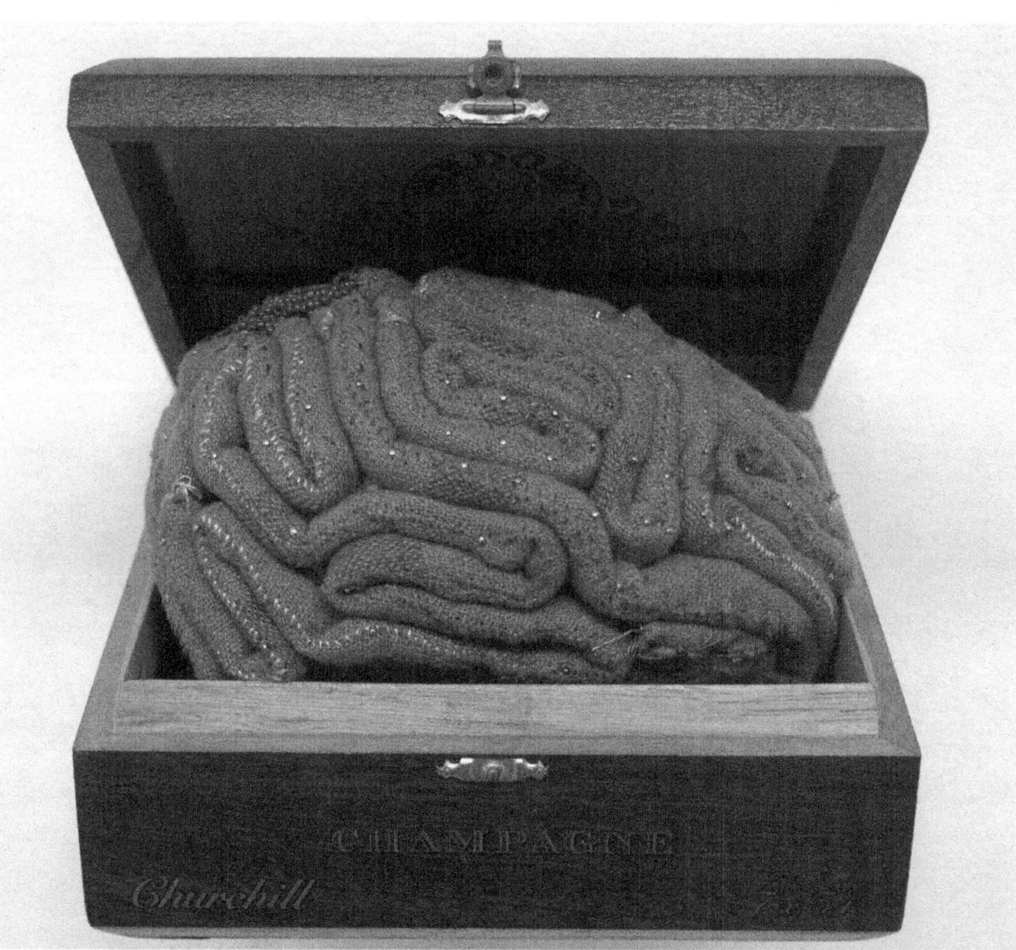
CHAMPAGNE
Churchill

Part Three:

The time-traveling inventor disinvents himself.

Selfless, selfless, ungrateful child

I've spent nothing but time doing nothing but service. Doubt me?
Where would you be without
The quivering jump of the second hand,
Without the pop and rush of an opening
Umbrella?

I have never made or done a thing for me alone.

Even a saunter around the grounds affects the lives of beetles and field mice, of
molecules and particles, of trees. Perhaps the very design of my hike required me to
perambulate to the north by northeast whilst ruminating on the unexplored
territory of the underwater caves of my property, thus removing my attention, thus
forcing me to grind my heel on the carapace of one iridescent creature after another.
I was meant to kill.
Or be killed.
And no one pays me enough attention to afford me that relief.

My intentions have granted me freedom from paranoia.
Now I welcome raisins in my mush. So what if they are shadows of fingerprints?

Guess I'll go eat worms

It is only selfish if
there is someone who needs you.
Somebody had to concoct self-pity; all it took was berating
homo erectus.

I am a million years old, so many time-miles have elapsed 'neath my pumping
thighs; I am an autumn cock, riding passage like a lynx, like the purpled lips of a
strangled victim straining to etch legacy on the world, like a father.

Banal time philosophies exist to comfort the dying. What I wouldn't give for a
natural cause. A there's nothing else.

Peaches, you slither in the periphery. I cannot decipher your drool; without my
tender irrigation, a crusty cap has formed over your teardrop nostrils, bilious
stalagmites climb from lip to lip. What's it like over there? Same old, same old.

Minister to me. Afford me the same courtesy I extended you.
You were always good at nothing. Sit on my face,
there's a good feather pillow.

Poison at night, sailor's delight

Every time the doctor comes
near me, I get ether.
It's not like I don't have my own supply, but
ether is like eggs:
always better when someone else cooks it.

Hallucinations can't kill you. But you can kill you. Resolve, that slippery beast,
transforms to grease, and there I am, once again, at the nadir of a spiral staircase,
bellowing commands at specters: Fire that dusty musket; slit my veins.
Lucky for me, it always eventually turns out your ghosts are you.

Poison comes naturally; my body manufactures as long as I feed. Needles come
naturally; men have always wanted a way to go beyond the flesh casing, and then we
craved salted sausage. My serology topography is wiggly and nonsensical, just like
my sweet Peaches' brains.

An orange at night will kill you. A plum in the morning will assist with regularity.
Best to stay away from muesli at midday, and lay off the sauce completely. All day
long, I stimulate my kidneys with tantalizing admixtures of dust and oil, flour and
spittle. Those submissive enough to walk behind me observe my organs
rhythmically bumping 'gainst my cummerbund.

Overriding the systems: That's the hush-hush.
I can shut anything down. I created my body, and I can destroy it. Tout de suite.
Blood, phlegm, bile, mucus, wax, meninges: I bathe in raw weasel meat.
There is more than one way to die.

I manmade death.

Consumption seems to be the only way
out. I cannot imagine a time when my cheeks
were not chipmunked, when my belly did not
distend beyond my trousers' gentle truss.
I invented elastic. I invented excess.

I invented life. All it took was a touch of glitter. But this is the thing that will
hopefully kill me. It was already invented. It did not matter. Even bananas can do
it. The air is thick with flies.

My stinky pile. Lemon curd and blood clots, enamel and succulent capillaries: You
are like a beaten egg. You are like chewing gum stretching betwixt sole and
pavement. You are like me. My miscarriage. My blood baby. My stinky pile.
Care for me.

Smear your stain over my parted maw, and enter me. Suck my tongue as you slide
over cilia and under uvula. My gag reflex is just that, a reflex: Don't let it thwart
intentions, yours or mine. Enter me.

Rip my spleen, rattle my gall, burden my kidneys, overwhelm my liver, and
snuggle down into the curve of my appendix. Remain there till the liquid
escapes its casing, till you can feel my palms rubbing and grabbing
at you through layers of gristle and cake.
Kill me.

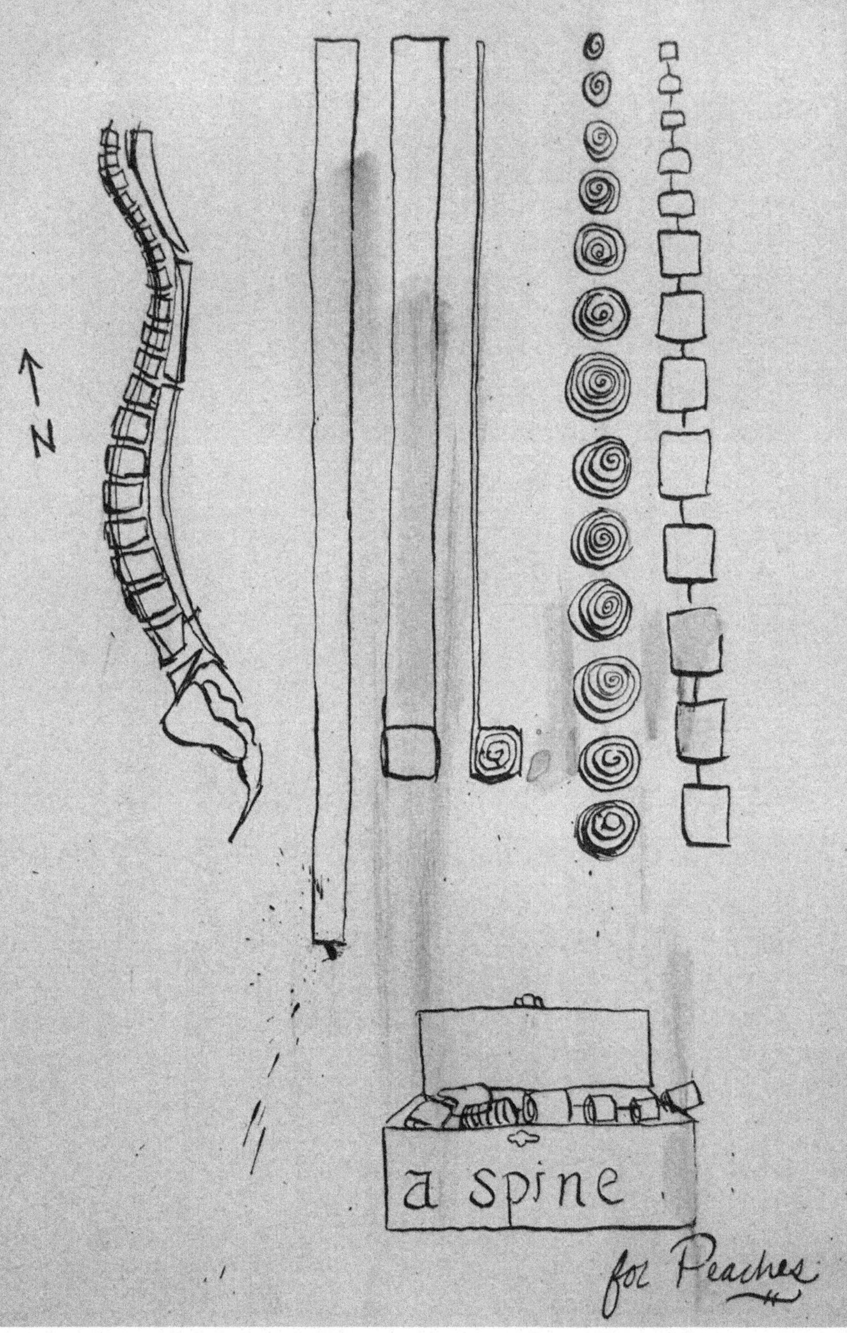

N
a spine
for Peaches

Tough Skin

Your drunken uncle doesn't sleep

The field of medicine has not yet yielded a visionary
confident enough to replace human eyes with rat mouths,
or just get the damn thing done with and remove the nose
entirely. Noses are the new appendices.

Kip asked a plastic surgeon to graft a dying
elephant's trunk onto her shoulder, and he refused.
Is it the asymmetry, or the cross-species procedure?
Did she offend his artist's eye, or his surgeon's ethic?
Possibly it's that he'd have to involve a neurologist
so the trunk wouldn't droop immobile.
Pride is usually the culprit.

This is what you had in mind: There are faces
everywhere, and not just on humans, but animals, too,
and one person I know who had a powerful
electron microscope told me even
dust has a face.

It's beady and mean.
It looks like your drunken uncle waiting up for you.

What if you fell in love with that uncle and he
died, and then you made your husband get a little plastic
globe inserted under the skin on the bridge of his
nose to approximate the loose cartilage of your beloved's?

People want people to look like other people all the time.
You are probably not sick.

Why do you think I never wear mascara?

Imagine you are Humphrey Bogart.
Imagine those bags, the way they'd feel
when you rolled them between your fingertips.
Like pinching a snake.

Not even the hundred-year-old monkey, eating
with chopsticks like a real boy, can stomach your
self-indulgence. He makes a gesture that you figure
you can interpret later, after you've
learned a little bit more.

We should always be staring
at those ugly men and women, horrified
at their largeness. I would be there now,
gazing and clutching, longing for a mate
with bow lips and jaundice. My teeth
would fleck away in translucent scales,
so many smiles would I make.

Oral hygienists would sew together the tissue
of corpses to bring a shade down over my exposed
nerves. A cigarette would jangle me up into the sky
until I was sitting on my ugly man's sloped shoulders
thinking about how nice it is to cry
in front of someone without caring
about how you look.

Pore to pore

You will never be smooth, not even if I cover you
in another creature's skin. You are getting
old, but you hold onto your youth in the form of
blackheads.

The problem is I don't like to measure.
Maybe you should do it yourself.
I am not talking about making a human skinsuit. Nothing
tailored. Just...find some carcasses and
clean them. Just... make a cape--no
buttons or zippers necessary, only arm
holes and mouth holes.

Did I ruin everything when I suggested he wasn't
bare-chested? The worst part about the hirsute is
they don't lick themselves so smells get
trapped in the furry arcs like a fart
in bed or maybe the worst part is people
don't want humans to smell like hundred-year-old monkeys.

Fruit and flower, not mammal or fish.
I think I ate crab disguised as cheese today. Your face
would have caught it and filled in your pores until your skin
couldn't breathe any more and you died like a frat boy
covered in house paint. Even the soles of his feet.

I will make you a living statue, and forget
to oil your joints, and then you will be mine mine
mine. I will hang necklaces I never
wear from your fingers and rub chapstick on
scaly body parts.

If it seems like you are cold, like for instance
if your eyes roll back, I will put my mouth against
your skin and breathe.

How people die

Nobody knows what's in them woods.
Probably ain't no ghost beavers or hundred-year-old monkeys, but
The Clicker might be using his long, skinny
legs as camouflage, his plate face shimmering.
His mouth is a crack.

The fish with a thousand feelers walks only in
reverse on the sand ground of the ocean.
The child molester lurks behind the porch swing.
Your drunken uncle just took a swig of the bottle of wine
represented by a darker swatch of green in the
forefront of the view, and now he's fallen
asleep in the ditch that is represented by a subtle black line.

If you didn't know it was there you would
think it was nothing but rolling hills and blue jays, but
surprise surprise there aren't even swallows, and every
single blade of grass has an ant on it.
The ants are harmless.
You might harm them though.

Sometimes people look at paintings and think
about how nice it is when the water or the mountain
graduates into the sky, but think of the real-life
consequences if you were sitting on top of the mountain,
and then which parts were mountain and which parts were sky
became fuzzy.
That is how people die.

How much do you hate me?

It is difficult to be treated
shabbily, and that is why
people usually adopt puppies
instead of dogs.

Look, you can grind me
to pulp and press me into a cut-out
of exactly the same size and shape
as my body. I will be like a really
big cookie that smells of off
meat.
You can eat the less gristly bits
every Tuesday as a way to stave
off returning to the grocer and
buying all those boxes you like.
You can drink my
runoff in your bloody
marys.

Isn't my willingness to submit
to violence adorable?
Don't you find yourself
softening toward me even now?

The hundred-year-old monkey loses his touch

Did you hear that time isn't linear, so that is
why you are having those dreams.
I did eat raspberries with you tomorrow.
I did feel rejected when your own hand
seemed more interesting to you than my red face.

Your fingers were stained with chocolate, but I was holding
an entire raisin oatmeal cookie in my mouth
for fear of making a wet swallowing sound.

My cheeks were rounded and should have made
you think of sex. That is what rounded things do.

Just ask the hundred-year-old monkey
who won't stop playing with your
mostly deflated balloon.
He can't make an animal anymore.
He forgot to play sodoku.
He forgot to meet new people.
Sometimes he cuddles now, accidentally.

Your middle distance makes me think of myself,
just like everything else: my fingers
perpetually stained blue from cold,
nails like a heart attack.
I can tell I am getting older because no
one ever attempts to transfer warmth with
their own body parts.

Even the drunken uncle avoids my outstretched thumb
for sucking, watching the suggestion
of ceiling fan blades reflected in his glasses,
substituting pudgy legs with loose hamstrings scissoring the air.

I spit up like a baby, but it smells much worse.

Stacking the dead

You keep telling me to have
fun as if you think I am not,
but I am well put together.
My dead are stacked neatly.
My conscience is clear.

I could be in touch with my emotions.
I could mop the floor or go to the post office or drink juice.

I could stand underneath a precariously placed object.
I could eat a handful of fur.
I could teach you how to puke.

Do you remember we used to wear boots because they were easy? Do you
remember when you bought all those black cats and trained them to walk zigzags in
front of you?

I would nibble the salt from your sweaty
dehydrated face and spit it back
into your mouth to keep you going, just for me.
A piebald animal watches us always, and he
doesn't even have the decency to shrink into shadows.
He will not let us tell each other the truth and even now sticks
his fingers in my mouth so you gag.

There's a patch of blue forming in the wrong place,
and the magnetic force between the drunken uncle
and the fat-bottomed baby is attractive.
Don't worry:
He is only going to gently cradle her and turn pop songs to lullaby.
He thinks he loves her.

The pathology of people

I can never tell why you are yelling at me, or how, when I deserve
to be yelled at you're somehow not there and instead there is a patch of blue.

Kip is going back to school to participate in an experimental
program, and her thesis will center on the pathology of people
who need to go back to school. She will turn all the data she gathers
inward, her brain a-swirl with tales of lost husbands and
cats, until her large intestine ruptures and she has a
near-death experience. Then she will
study that. She will have excellent
numbers on the internet because her romantic story
counteracts her monotone.

I will hold her office hours in the master
bathroom, staring at the dropped
ceiling and wondering if the attic is jam-packed with
insulation or squirrels. Anyone could find patterns
in the dots, so I will look for words.
All I will find is god.
No one will think I am wasting my time.

Maybe I would have been a good
journalist, and you should have been a carpenter.
I could have made up puns all day, and you could have built
cradles that were really coffins.

I am the drunken uncle crouched in the crawl
space, frustrated with time and chemical reactions.
I am going to touch your peter pan
collar, and you are going to slap me.
You will become hysterical after I drop to the
ground, but I am not really hurt.
I am waiting for you to crouch so I can ogle your
triangle. You will insert your high heel in my
you-know-what,
but everything about me proves to be more
resilient than either of us imagined.

It is good we touched your collar.
It is good you were there to witness it.
If it wasn't your collar we touched, it might have been
someone else's, who wouldn't have been able to handle it.

Squeezebox

Clever little monkey, quick
with a quip and an eye
flick to prove he gets it, too.
You got it too
long ago, and now it seems easier
to navigate the space within your
shared square than to laugh hollowly
as a businessman. Clip and paste
the good times till a man
with a tomato nose appears, and
you know the sum of a thousand million
pieces of confetti. The too-bad part
is the flame-retardant wax coating.
Pick up a handful, mold an organ, and play
it till all the air squeezes from your lungs,
leaving you without
any danger in your body.

Rub it on your lips

I would have gone along if nature
had something more to say than
peace. I wish peace were
something you could peel.
But if it weren't boring it wouldn't
be peace. Stop saying peace.
Eat an onion like an apple.
Cut and rub a hot pepper on your
mucous membranes.

I didn't go though, and it didn't
make any difference. Butterfly wings, my ass.
There is very little significance in the act of piling
one's hair high upon the head. Oh, but I love the deep
ache of pulling it out after a long day.
It is even better when you do it.

I saw a feverfew flower lying bruised in
front of the stackable washer-dryer.
I attached loneliness to it.
You saw my bloody thumbnail by the
doorjamb and assumed horror.
I just thought it was too hard.
It wasn't representative of my being as a whole.

I will paint you with your mouth open.
Your bloody gum gaps I'll fill
with little tooth-baring monsters.
Give them some beef jerky.
They love chewing by proxy.

Fear and bad breath awakens the
hundred-year-old monkey who watches you
sleep and reports back to your drunken uncle.
The monkey knows you can't sleep on your side.
It is not just the threat of undue pressure on the
heart; it is the possibility of losing love in comfort.

Don't look behind you

He's out there. Sure as you're born.
One second you'll be walking down
the street and the next—beatific chaos.
Your brain will freaking light up.
You'll look around to try to finger the trigger, and whammo:
a little girl who looks exactly like me, except her sundress is
redder than her face, and her hair is naturally curly. You will take
her hand, and she will notice the light in your eyes and feel unafraid.

But it is always when you are happiest that
the hundred-year-old monkey peels his lips back
to display gaps and yellow wood.
His finger feels like a tongue when he sticks it in your ear.
You can't recoil or he'll pierce your eardrum.
Now you are his puppet.

You're always popping out of the crawlspace
wielding a chainsaw and a speculum.
You drink vivid sodas.
You know when the full moon will come.
You are always a little bit stuffed up.

Oo ee oo ah ah, you say,
and she smiles at you, all gaps and pearl.
You are afraid to pet her;
you have no idea how to re-attach hair.

Your cats are right

The root of the word "raptor" is "rapt,"
or "wrapped," which means when
someone puts their mouth around your head.
Butter isn't naturally yellow, and cheese
isn't natural. It is a conspiracy constructed
by the Dutch, who want to lull you
with their ability to use the letter
"a" many times in a row in a word.
Every word is like a sigh.
The root of the word "owl" is "ow,"
a shortened version of the word "couch,"
which many people say instead of "sofa."
"Ow" is not a plosive, even though it can
sometimes be said to explode from sphincters.
You have to be careful with household items,
especially the vacuum cleaner. Your cats are right.
It might suck off your big toe, and then
any sense of balance you ever had will be forever lost.

Slow motion murder

The Clicker does not have a plate face.
It has a ladyhead, and lobster claws for hands.
When it runs it makes a sound like corduroy.
Its mouth is a crack.

Kip wants the plastic surgeon to reattach her
tongue now, but he forgot to play sodoku
so his hands tremble uselessly and he can only
remember his calico cat's name,
Mr. Dribbles, which is something he says often,
appropriately, as he moistens his fingers with his
tongue and does impressions of your drunken uncle
with his legs in the stirrups.

You did not kill anyone, not really, because everyone
commits tiny murders every day in slow motion
so as not to be detected. I know several people who
have taken a cheesegrater to your drunken uncle's earlobes
when he is about to pass out.

They all wear masks of your face.
That explains a lot, doesn't it?

His drunken eyes see you you you in everyone—
his wife, your mother, his plastic surgeon, your daughter.
Your husband watches the two of you, as Richard
Nixon and Humphrey Bogart, tongues protruding
from mask mouth holes, touching and retreating,
swelling, shriveling, dying.

His nose and earlobes keep growing,
and nothing can be done. Not even the
hundred-year-old monkey is immune. Not even you.

You touched the tip of his nose with the tip
of your finger and your nail grew into an
unmanageable curl that hurt when you clipped it.
This dark matter is repulsive.
His diseases are catching.

A perfect man

Your drunken uncle likes to make macramé
owls and then shove planters in their mouths.
My drunken uncle likes to make
sweet love and then fall asleep.

If only we could combine the two to make a perfect man!

Did you know that every single human being on the planet
has a drunken uncle, real or imaginary? Sometimes
those uncles are mothers and sometimes they are picnic baskets.

I like to macramé drunken uncles,
using Styrofoam balls as their heads and balls.
I like to look at the hooked needle and dream
about piercing my thigh, my buttock, the ball of my foot.

If someone left me alone long enough I would learn
how to properly spice your meals.
I'd clean the windows and finally get some
replacement bulbs. I'd start to spin secrets
that nobody else cared about, and then I'd make
up a drunken uncle with stubble to run from.

Got your tongue

First I will cut off your tongue,
and next I will press a teddy bear
stamp into one
of those multi-colored ink pads, and squish
it onto that detached and meaty muscle for long
enough and with enough
pressure that it looks like an angel
or an atom
when I pull away.

The pressure will probably make it bleed
out the back, so I will lay down newspapers.
I never read them anyway.
Do you want the newspapers, too?
I could send them to you when I send your tongue.
It's no big deal.

I am not doing this because of some obvious desire
to shut you up. I have always liked the way you
sound when you moan.

Additionally, there are certain schools
of yogic thought that believe the tongue
is the root of tension in the body.

You are probably firmly pressing it to the roof of your mouth right now.

I am also interested in decay.
Will it smell like a dead mouse behind a radiator,
or more like roast beef greening in the sun?
Will it shrivel or swell?

I can pass along my research to serious
science journals, and readers will learn about
how much time can elapse before the body rejects
an organ. It would be so cool if, after I cut it off,
your body would try to take it back,
like if I placed your tongue back in your mouth
and a little flesh fist erupted out of your throat
and grabbed the severed edge,
holding everything back together till it fused.

But you are far too passive for something like that to occur.

Big wet one

It is only the unloved that live forever.
They have less chance of contact
with passion. Coincidence that the
hundred-year-old monkey is a virgin?
That's difficult to pull off in monkey world.

When your husband says your drunken uncle is
starting to grow on him you know that the time has come.
Either he will start drinking a handle of scotch
whiskey a day, or he will kick your drunken uncle in the
torso with such vigor that a floating rib detaches
and lodges itself in his lung. Your drunken uncle is
too frail to handle such abuse.

You guide him through familiar motions,
moving his tongue in and out and around.
You look for pampas grass or clover for the
dumping but find only solid cement bags,
and you are unsure how to make pavement.

The monkey emerges and you think it's to help you—
he's been a bit of a turncoat throughout the years—
but then you see he loves you, too.

He wants to plant a big wet one on you.
You are too easy to love, and there are
consequences for everything. You will get caught.

Babies can't cry underwater

I've never seen anything
like it. The babies
flock to you like a murder:
disturbed and dressed in black,
their chubby hands stirring vats
of dye, dropping in bonnets
and booties, murmuring poetry
they still remember from the other side.
Who can have disturbed them, other than
their drunken uncles? They think his nose
is a horn—beep beep!

Their nails like transparent tape, too weak
to draw blood; their hair like angel
fur without the bite. You gather
them like so many pine cones in
a sack and toss them in the river.
The water boils because of a conflagration
of rattle-dry reeds in an air pocket below.
There is a scientific reason for everything.

You love too hard, so you have to hate
too hard for balance. You cry way too much,
which produces ripples in your outer field of vision.
A baby head pops out of the concentric circles every
now and again to wink at you.
You did the right thing.

You always do the right thing.
These babies would have made
their nannies nutso and seriously cut
into their TV time.
Still, when the decay becomes more
apparent, you curse your adaptability
and pray for a long arm to circle
your waist and yank you under.

Rattlesnake on the bed

The Midwife

Midwife I

One thousand four-leaf clovers plus a vine of sweet peas makes it healthy. Gather
the clovers by the light of a full moon. If even one three-leaf clover makes it into
your haul, that baby is fucked, limbless. You can get the sweet pea vine from your
local greenhouse.

Rub lavender pebbles from the health food store wholesale bins onto the mother's
ripe tummy. Pour hydrogen peroxide and erase that weird line that bisects the
lower half-circle, turning babies into sour peaches with hard, wrinkled centers. Send
the lady to the salon, for general upkeep and removal of the business down there.
Then, pray a full rosary with the dough-faced nun that keeps watch over the world
from her perch on public television.

Make small talk: Any day now, any day, pretty lady. Full head of hair! Two little
eyeteeth!

Never, ever say 'parasitic twin.' Reassure. Do not say 'gnawed nipples.' Especially
do not giggle after you've said it.

Gather the instruments: metal tongs, four sets of tweezers (pointy, not pointy, spare
not pointy, blue (pointy or no, no matter)), good book, boiling water (best to keep a
pot on at all times), pottery jug filled one quarter of the way with goat's blood (milk
will do in a pinch), kerosene lamp, clean cloth, shiny brass door knob, and a potato.

I don't know what the fuck I'm doing.

Midwife II

These are the way babies get born: square, seal-shaped, doubled, trebled, people-shaped, red-headed. Wormy and way too small.

"Oh, the possibility!"

She smiles and begins an exercise I prescribed in her third month. She traces a cylinder over and around her poky belly button. It will awaken awareness in the baby of its journey down the chute of life. So I said.

"Will her eyes be blue?" she says, dreamily. Also I make her thump out, on her belly, the rhythms I learn from my steel drum class. It increases intelligence and grace. The baby will never need spectacles.

Its eyes best be blue, or this be the milkman's child. So said the peas. "Oh, yes, oh, yes."

Things I know, I repeat.

I close my eyes and feel around inside of her, warm and riddled with stalactites. The inside is pink when I shine my flashlight.

"A girl."

Or a boy. You know, as long as it isn't jaundiced or epileptic or dead.

What I lack in my kit: a pair of scissors. The child's head rents a jagged path between birth canal and that other, dirty hole. Squashy potato head, plugged with slime. It shoots out like a star, and there I am holding a whole child I did not hurt.

I am prescient. I am a born midwife. I have to quit before I kill someone.

Midwife III

I have written a bestseller: *The New Child: Borne of Gristle and Hair, Stewed in Musk.* Okay, so it actually isn't a true bestseller in the sense that its principle audience is comprised of mad scientists and kindly women. There aren't many mad scientists, and the women are afraid to read it in public lest they be labeled quirky.

Also, I am told the reptilian brain is inherently frightened of the title; it seems smelly.

But I will not change it.

The basic tenet: Conventional wisdom states that children are made of people—but you can totally create your own with everyday objects. And then there are instructions.

Gather. We have been doing it for long before we even knew to be afraid of rats. Gather like an addict scraping precious dust from foil and grout. Hard children are made of dog whiskers, men's toenail clippings (the yellower the better), and spittle.

Sperm does play a role, but it is very slippery. Recommended that you put it in a receptacle directly. Like your vagina.

But if you want a soft child, it is far more difficult to attain. It is not made of love, you fucking sap. It is made of goose down, your grandmother's biscuits, and lead paint.

Birth is like being pitched from a great height into a shallow lake, except the opposite--a splash into a cold so sharp it takes your breath away. Don't feel bad if your baby comes out blue; that's the luckiest thing, not ever having to breathe.

Midwife IV

Yesterday this baby plopped into my palms with an hourglass figure: eensie breasts spurting droplets of milk, hips swiveling as she effortlessly assumed the lotus position. She could hold her head up right away. Her eyes had something behind them, and it was immediately clear she would not need sleep till midnight.

Fearing the next step (an even smaller fully formed woman popping out of her nether regions, and then an even smaller one from that even smaller one and on and on until they were just invisibly small fully formed women giving birth to one another into infinity), I plugged her up, put her in my pocket and took her to Chile.

Deep in the jungle there is a miniature forest that protects kittens fierce as jaguars and mini-horses with joints that actually move. The trick to finding it is looking closely.

My baby-woman seemed overwhelmed, and her pelvic area was bloated, stretching and mottling the skin. I looked at her in my magnifying mirror that I use to tweeze my eyebrows and observed her gooseflesh.

Really, she had a far better chance of finding that cute little land than I ever did. I gave her a shove with my index finger and off she scuttled. I watched until I saw her harness a millipede and ride off on it through the underbrush. That was pretty gross.

At night I say a prayer. Prayers don't all have to be to the same God or even use the words thee or thine. I say I love the Universe and everything and everybody in it. These will be my last words. These will be my last words.

The Candystriper

Candystriper I

They will let anybody in here. They will suit them up and propel them toward coffee machines bigger than those old computers that took up whole foyers.

The uniforms are fucking attractive. I'm a milkmaid, a mermaid, a lover of order and kindness and order again. My hat is so very starchy: hot-cha.

They make me put on gold lipstick in the ladies'; I imagine it to be *de rigeur* until I notice the others' lips gone gooey and naked.

Forty-seven people I touched have died. We get our thirty thousand beats, and when they're done, yowza. Look out, old people, it is a day to die. Young people, too, let's drink coffee till our lips quiver and shoot spittle into the crevasse.

The smell of liver makes me vomit a pale, fleshy crescent into the water cooler, and the nurses join hands to push me out of their fold. They do not do anything. They talk to each other. That is all. The phone rings and rings until the sound of it stops being a sound at all and becomes a feeling like that time when you came home from school and no one was there.

Towels, fighting with their looped white fibers, their stiff odor and the promise that things can be wiped: I hang them.

What do you mean, I don't get paid?

Candystriper II

The bulging apron drives old women to distraction. They stare into space and murmur platitudes like *everyone's got an envelope to stuff*. I have more than one, more than ten thousand; I have days of envelopes. Nothing satisfies their empty space.

So, the men wear vests and take longer breaks, which pleases everyone. They come back smelling of dark smoke, cut their meatball fingers on sharp flaps and bleed all over the pleas.

Inevitably blood wanders over to my double-Ds, and there I am, as usual, covered in handprints. A nurse lends me her teddy bear scrubs, and next thing I know masked people yell STAT, and I totally get it. I hand over the scalpel. I flush pus. I am an extension of genius.

Adrenaline is better than pancakes or pain killers. Ask anyone who's ever lifted a bus.

Ministering to others makes me feel like a nun who has a lot of really excellent sex with rich men who buy me golden jewelry. How could this possibly get any better?

In the end, it just don't matter how good you are at intubating someone. You got to have paper.

Candystriper III

Me oh my but a gal can striate sweets anywhere. I am young, uneducated and promiscuous: The world is my hospital.

Everywhere you go, people licking internal lacerations, their cries for help garbled by busy tongues. It usually doesn't take much more than a well-placed slit to alleviate pressure. My scalpel understands.

"Where does it hurt?"

The man looks Mayan or Sioux, once he untangles his legs from his arms and the shrubbery. His cheekbones rival my blade for edge, so after his breathing calms, I ask him to join me, traipsing cross-country, spreading joy by letting blood.

He shakes his head like that will help: "I am without gifts, *mon cheri*, powerless, desexualized, and without country."

We'll see about that.

Fifteen minutes later, Pedro and I are in love.

Then, like the rest of them, he starts talking: about fire and smelt and the ladies. I am not the jealous type, so I can't really understand why I slice the hinges of his lips, exposing corn-rows of pink-tinged molars.

I think he might still love me. I'm not quite sure what to do about that.

The Chaperone

Chaperone I

The bad girls parade up and down the beach in their striped string bikinis. To join them, I have to turn my back.

Tiny cottages house the girls and their watchers, three apiece, one to a bed, all on the up and up. I slide in with the right forms and a history of care. Dutifully, I shake my head.

I observe as they flagellate each other with seaweed and dunk the unsuspecting. One time, I am victim, perched as cheerful as a swallow on pool's rim. My eyes sting when I break the surface again: I cannot trust them. Also, my eyes sting from chlorine, not realization or tears, asshole.

Twelve compliments, two human touches per day for each young lady. I pay quarters instead of kind words at the arcade, and when they win twisted glass pop bottles filled with mysterious neon liquids, that works, too. They lift and reverse.

The drugstore causes problems: Permanent solutions permitted, but peroxide rinses not.

All their names are Kim and Lisa and they want to go to Long John Silver's for their birthday dinners. I sing Christmas hymns in the van to cheer them, but my favorite tune is melancholy, and it works only in the sense that they laugh at me.

We build a sheer membrane between us. They blacken their lashes with match dust and cut their fingers. I sleep soundly, unaware of my impending break.

Chaperone II

Is it okay to give the girls peach slices? Toe rings? Back rubs?

The rollercoaster is so old there are no restrictions. Babes can ride in mothers' arms.
The elderly need only set their wheelchairs on the track and hitch on as a caboose.
If you can dream it, you can do it.

"Bullshit," Kim says and wedges her hips so bone rubs bone. I want to push her
over the edge.

A sign announces we have passed the point of no return. "We should stand up." It
doesn't go upside down. Besides, there is a little thing called physics.

The keening springs from me as we sail over and under flaking paint, and I really
don't blame her reaction. These lips are built for talking. Her ear feels like a dried
apricot between my teeth. Skin-and-bones, daisies in her mouth.

I did not, did not, did not do it. Just because you think of something doesn't mean.

Those who entered: Ten bad girls, two chaperones, a breath of fresh air and a
butterfly big as a gull. We all exited, too, excepting that some of us were
transformed—and isn't that the yearning?

I drank the last of the wine. I neglected to lock the back door. I did not pick up
after myself. I forgot that others make the decisions.

Don't let anyone tell you sleeping on the sand is romantic.

Chaperone III

Nobody admits this unless you beat your fists on their chest, but it turns out work defines you. Hunter, gatherer, chaperone. I scrape skins. I bead. I am so utterly broken and innocuous that I should be trusted to do anything by anyone.

Living on a rollercoaster is exactly as you would imagine. Your hair never looks right, and you get hand cramps. People mistake me for a safety officer and bullhorn complaints as I whip past.

"My mascara ran when the rushing air caused my eyes to tear!" "I lost my flip-flops!" "Whiplash!" "My little girl jumped out at the crest of the hill, and now she's holding on by her soft pink little girl fingernails from the structure and I'm afraid she's going to fall and die!" "Vomit!"

Rescuing the clinging children brings the greatest satisfaction; those that stay behind and ride beside me, holding my hand—well, the rushing air, mascara, etc. Caregivers fetch and carry cheese fries and fried dough. I subsist.

Kim and Lisa come through occasionally, but our relationship has changed. I am clear now, airborne. They say I am the most comfortable seat.

I am ready to take the next step into perpetual movement. I am ready for my brain to stop and my body to keep going. There is, apparently, a void, which frightens people because it's tough to think about something that is nothing.

But I have been thinking about nothing for so long.

Chaperone IV

When a rollercoaster runs off the rails, you get shot into outer space. First step is everything you consume tastes like rancid butter: funnel cakes, corn dogs, everything. Second, rancid butter sensory hallucination seems like a celestial blessing in retrospect because you've ballooned to twice your size.

Space debris whips my cheeks and rips my clothing. Everything looks like a granite countertop on large scale: swirly and chock full of minerals. It's like a condominium kitchen disintegrated in my direction.

It only gets really bad when the half of my body facing the sun bubbles and fries, and the dark half freezes. Frozen skin is way gross, like meat, which I suppose it actually is. The only part that feels good is a single stripe down the middle of my body.

This is the way I end. Probably. I can't be certain. It is difficult to know my mind without other minds knocking into it. Is it wrong to wish for companions when enduring extreme pain?

When I hated you I was thinking of you. I thought of the way your eyes really did seem like bedrooms, and the way your nose could have been a ski slope if I was miniature, or you were huge. When I loved you I was thinking of you.

Everybody speculates about death, and it turns out it's a lot like life. So, so boring.

The Babysitter

Babysitter I

When the kids lock themselves in the closet, this is your opportunity to ready the house for the fooling. Four o'clock becomes nine-thirty when shades seal out the light. Pop in a tape of Johnny Carson, and eyelids droop.

Children often don't wear underwear to bed. That is wrong.

Go ahead and smoke the butts in the ashtray. You cannot get herpes from a filter. Syphilis, though, if you embrace the dolphin in the shoebox on the uppermost shelf.

Tell them it's your time to play, should they discover the daylight. Convince them they are dream-bound by swaying a lot so as to mess with their as-yet-matured vision, and if they don't go back to bed…well, best they watch themselves.

Catch syphilis in the early stages, penicillin makes you good as new. Let it fester and you get The Swiss Cheese Brain. Get a shot in the buttock every couple months and you can do whatever you want.

Eventually, the parents come back. You cannot escape the parents.

Exact your revenge when the wee ones awaken at three o'clock in the morning, clamoring for sugar cereal.

You are long gone. You are drunk.

Babysitter II

Even if you do not steal the silver dollars or burn down the gazebo, you will get
blamed for it.

Repeat business and reputation are overrated; you will do just fine when you choose
to dust shelves with your sleeve pulled over your hand. Others will trail you with a
bottle of bleach.

So she asked for balloons and all they had was condoms. It's not like she asked for
wine and I gave her grappa. I did not feed her the sciatic nerve.

So she asked where her father was, and I told her I did not know. She had blue eyes.
He did not. So she asked the meaning of life. Life has nothing to do with life.

How was I to know? If little girls are allergic to earthworms and asphalt, then
tackle football is clearly out of the question.

Swollen like a biddy, lift-off seemed imminent; I twined her ankle to a branch.

Ways in which the present can destroy the future: admission, broken necks,
friendship, integrity, anaphylactic shock, trust.

I heard she lived.

Babysitter III

Mi amor, mi charge-o. Mi Pedro.

I do not mean this in a sick way, but children have the nicest skin. It's like fabric.

He's really far too old for babysitting. This woman in a modified nurse's uniform saw my ad, dropped him off on my doorstep. She appeared distraught.

Honey, I said, you do not have to tell me about trauma. I was about to go on and on and on, but she brandished a knife at me and went click-clacking in her stilettos down my driveway. She had really big boobs.

Somehow he retains child skin. He will not go to bed.

"I am lovelorn, see?" he says.

"Si," I say. But I don't really know Spanish.

I do know this: It is always good to offer men and children food. I root around my kitchen for wheat crackers or lollipops or turkey clubs, but come up bereft. When I return to the sofa to cradle his head while inducing night terrors, he is vanished.

"My darling," the note says. "I must not let the devil beat me. Gone to 7-Eleven for a Quaffer, then to find the loves of my life. I will not skywrite. It results in injury."

I am included in that plural. I am loves.

Babysitter IV

My momma didn't hesitate to rub rye on my gums when I fussed. My father once
took his belt off and set it in the curled position of a rattlesnake on the bed.

Corporal punishment sounds like something the military lays on you, the way a
guilt trip sounds like a cheery car ride through a mother's psyche. I beat the shit out
of the Chaperone as a young girl, but believe you me, that little bitch deserved it.
You can't lay nothing on me.

She always craved something. Happiness lies in the absence of desire; I whipped the
want from her.

A weepy child—all of her orifices stank of dirt: She was a product of her birth. My
momma dug a hole deep in the forest, where the witches and hidden indigenous
creep. She squatted and sang pain until that twisted knot of a child plopped face
first into the mud of the pit. Its first mouthful of earth spake its future.

Little sisters are terrible things, perversions of the original. What is a chaperone
anyway, if not Babysitter Lite? Diet Babysitter?

Babysitter V

I don't need to see your face up close to remember the boring fizz of love. My memory is far superior to any reality. Others' memories should not be considered.

You let me do things to you that no child should have to endure. You're my antidote, my prophylactic, my catalyst, my charge, and my savior all mushed into a man.

There are things about babies you have to learn. For instance, very small infants have alien immune systems. You don't know anything about what's happening on a cellular level unless you draw spinal fluid. You see, their memory is for shit, and they can't talk.

I feel like I am about to do something that I wouldn't do and so have become another person. Let me announce my intentions, Pedro. Come back to me. I promise to care for you in a traditional sense. I will buy wash cloths and products that promise no tears. I will not pervert and wield toys and sweets. I will love you so boringly that you enter a fugue state from which you will never emerge.

Hear my plea, or it's curtains.

Acknowledgments page

Many thanks to Megan Martin and Kathryn Regina, for kick-starting my writing again through collaboration. Some of their words appear embedded among my own in the third section of this book, as part of a different project we worked on together. Thanks also to Sarah Jackson-Moore, who had a conversation with me about horror imagery in art, out of which the second section of this book grew, and which in turn inspired her to create the artwork in this book. Thanks to Cooper Renner and *elimae* for publishing Midwife II (where it originally appeared). And thanks to Abby Rowold, as always, for lots of stuff.

Sarah Eaton's writing has appeared in various places around the internet, such as McSweeney's and elimae. She has a blog called The Grown-up. She works at Indiana University in Bloomington.

Made in the USA
Monee, IL
11 January 2026